SURVIVING PUPPY TRAINING

THE SIMPLE STEP-BY-STEP TRAINING BASICS AND TIPS FOR NEW DOG OWNERS

JADE STONE

CONTENTS

To all my family including Rex, Bruno, Whiteman, Grizzly, Chinny, and Stripes.

The pandemic has seen millions of pets adopted worldwide. Being home all the time with its inevitable boredom has forced many to finally keep that promise made eons ago that they would give a dog a great, loving home. We all know that having a dog can improve your life in many ways, therefore many took that plunge and went full-time into being doggie parents. A puppy though is a huge responsibility and you must be certain that you are ready to take on that job because puppies need a lot of affection and attention- yet with the very best of attention, they can be hard to control! Those cuties can cause a lot of "trouble" at home. Their energy is seemingly limitless, their little teeth find all the shoes in the house and they have little "accidents" on the carpet. Even when they get to the adult stage, they have to be carefully monitored too because of incessant or loud barking, digging holes on your perfectly manicured lawn, or pawing your friends as they enter your house. You must be ready for these things and more without pulling your hair out! Your puppy can be trained to be as good as he can be, and all the work and expenses you will experience as his parents are nothing compared to the joy, love, and true companionship he will return to you unconditionally.

1

SO YOU GOT A PUPPY!

So then, that energetic, loyal little bundle of joy (and sometimes exasperation) has already gotten all the family securely wrapped around their little paws, but can there be something you have forgotten? He is running around, barking happily and chewing everything in sight, but can he be ill without you knowing? He has gotten his shots you say, but there are so many other checks that need to be done to make sure little Rex is as healthy as he can be, and that he will enjoy a long life of happiness as an honorary part of your family. The fact is, there are hidden diseases that will only be uncovered with a full physical exam, and in truth if your vet has not mentioned this to you, you need to think about changing clinics. So many so-called "healthy dogs" have been brought to vets for shots or grooming and that expected, simple visit has turned up oral problems, heart murmurs, eye and joint anomalies, and many more conditions that were not suspected nor obvious. Most of the time, the owners are surprised, as they did not realize anything was wrong. This is why we are going to look at some of the most common issues that your vet will look out for when you take little Rex for his first appointment.

2

PUPPY'S FIRST VET APPOINTMENT

Your puppy should have a health check done by a vet by the time he is 6-8 weeks old. The vet will then decide how often he should visit, depending on the vaccination timetable that will be set up.

"Core vaccines are necessary and must be administered to puppies to protect them against adenovirus, parainfluenza, distemper virus, parvovirus, and rabies virus," Dr. Watkins says. " These vaccines may vary to some degree based on the region of the country you live in and what outbreaks have been seen in your area. These include Lyme disease, canine influenza H3N8 and H3N2, leptospirosis, and even rattlesnake vaccines."

Puppy vaccines are generally given on average at 8 weeks and booster shots are given three weeks apart. However, the rabies vaccine is mandatory in all states and has to be given at a minimum age of 4 months. You may also need to apply for a license once she has been vaccinated against rabies. (mandated by law!) A puppy must be licensed from age 4 months upward. This rabies license is an easy and most acceptable proof that doggie daycares and groomers need.

1. Meeting your dog

Just by observing, it may seem to you that your vet is just simply saying hi to your dog because he is just meeting him. However, what they are really doing goes much deeper than that. They are attentively assessing his general health. They are playing with Rex and also looking for behavioral issues like nervousness or aggression, eye and hearing issues, joint health and general mobility, brain function, coat and skin condition, and overall liveliness and spirit. It takes just one visit for your vet to immediately see if "something is wrong," which will cause him to look further, thus maybe saving your pet from pain, suffering, or even early death.

2. Mouth, nose, and throat

It is estimated that 80% of all dogs under three years old suffer from periodontal disease. This means that an oral exam for your dog is of utmost importance on any visit. A lot of congenital diseases can show up in the oral cavity. By looking at a puppy's tooth eruption pattern, one can also guess its age accurately. Its nasal discharge, whether clear or cloudy, often tells us too, that there is an infection or that your puppy is suffering from an allergy. Therefore, it is very important for these, and also his lymph nodes, to be checked thoroughly.

3. His eyes, ears, skin, and coat

You will notice that your vet will constantly run hands over your dog's skin. This is because its skin is its largest organ and thus will take priority in its checks. By closely observing your dog's coat and skin, the vet will see any sign of parasites, allergies, hygiene, any infection, its nutrition status, and also some inherited issues like growths and tumors. A radiant, shiny-looking coat is the first sign of a dog's health and gleaming, sparkling, intelligent eyes show suitable cognitive consciousness. A dog's skin or ears that are oily, flaky, dry, or dirty means that something is wrong and needs to be further checked.

4. Body condition score (BCS)

Your vet will want to set up a running weight and body condition score. This will make it easy for him to see any weight gain in time so that obesity does not occur, or he will see a sudden weight loss before it progresses further. If your dog is just a puppy, your vet will track his growth to ensure he is growing at the correct rate.

5. Spine and joints

Your vet will flex and extend your dog's knees, shoulders, hips, elbows, and spine to see if there is any pain, tenderness, or reduced motion. If your dog is a larger breed, this is especially important as they are at more risk of developing dysplasia, injuries of the spine, or any musculoskeletal issues.

6. Heart and lungs

Listening to your dog's heart with a stethoscope is a common and expected part of the exam. As simple and routine as it looks, however, it is one of the most important parts of the examination. This can warn of any respiratory infections, heart murmurs, and any incorrect anatomical development, thus ensuring a speedy investigation and treatment of any issue before it is too late.

7. The tummy

Your dog's tummy contains more important organs and essential tissues per square inch than any other part of her body. You will thus notice that your vet will be very unhurried and focused as he moves over his abdomen with his hands. This is very necessary during a check as this will show up any knot or hard spot or any other issues with his liver, spleen, kidneys, stomach, intestinal tract, or bladder before it snowballs into a bigger problem.

PUPPY EXPENSES

Your lovable little puppy while giving you joy, will also rack up some bills and most of these expenses will be in his first year. However, you will have to be prepared for recurring costs too. Let us look at the main ones:

How much does he cost?

If you are going to adopt your puppy, you may pay from nothing to over $500. This is dependent on the size and /or age of the puppy. If money is no object and you plan to buy a purebred, then you can be as much as $4000 in the hole financially.

Will you spay or neuter?

Most of the time, the cost of spaying or neutering the puppy will be added to the cost of adopting him. If you are buying a purebred again, however. Those costs will come from your pocket. The cost for these procedures usually costs from $200 to $500. The weight and size of the puppy determine this, to a large extent.

Veterinarians and vaccine shots

Your puppy's first set of vaccines will set you back about $50 to $300. Each vet appointment costs between $50 to $80.

Licenses and tags

The costs vary also and depend largely on where you live.

Tick, flea, and heartworm control

This will cost about $400 per year.

Food, feeding bowls, collars, leash, bedding, and other accessories

Food and treats for your puppy/dog will cost you about $80 each month. Collars and other stuff can cost very little or a whole lot. This is entirely up to your budget and what you are willing or able to spend.

Grooming

This can be very expensive but can also start at around $65 for each visit if your puppy is from a small breed. Larger breeds can cost up to $120 per visit. The time between grooming sessions is about 6 weeks.

Taking care of a puppy can also go beyond these costs. You also have to keep in mind the costs of doggie-daycares or boarding fees if you travel with him. The expenses that Rex incurs can indeed be high, but the total love and loyalty he gives in return make every dollar spent on him worth it!

PUPPY WOES!

Puppies are the cutest and most lovable little pets we can ask for. At the same time, they can be a lot of work, and if you are not prepared for the many needs, it can be a very exasperating time. Puppies can be almost as much work as a human baby and they are very time-consuming too as they have to be cared for, trained, entertained, and loved. All in all, as long as you ensure that you prepare well, your puppy will give you many years of great joy and happiness!

Below are some situations that will come up when you get a puppy and different ways you can get through them while having fun.

1. Crate training

This is a great tool for potty training, naps, and learning to be by themselves. Your pup will cry at first but will get used to the crate soon. A small pup can be in a crate for 30 -45 minute naps but can stay longer and longer as it grows. Your puppy's familiar toys and soft bedding will make the crate more comfortable and attractive. Never use the crate as punishment and never keep them inside for longer than their age needs. If you are going to be away all day, your dog can be placed in a closed-off area of the house or yard. He should be put back in the crate as soon as you return home.

2. Night crying

If your puppy is very young, he may not be able to hold his urine through the night. If he cries at night and wants to go, take him outside to relieve himself then place him in the crate immediately after.

Most vets say this is a good rule to follow: For every month in age your puppy has, he can hold it for one hour, then add one more hour. If a puppy is 3 months old for example, four hours at the most will most likely work for him. If this is not working, he needs to get checked by a veterinarian for a UTI or another issue. Always check his bedding as he needs to have clean dry bedding if it is soiled.

3. Oh lord...Diarrhea!

Puppies and poop problems go hand in hand! It is inevitable that your puppy will introduce you to this dreaded problem at some time or another. However, if he is having diarrhea for one whole day or more, or if he is also vomiting, get advice from your vet. It can be something more serious. You may also have to take in a sample to be tested so keep this in mind too.

4. Water! Water!

Your puppy must get clean, fresh water daily. He must be able to reach this water anytime he needs it. (Remember to hold it when it is near his bedtime)

5. Yes! Get that microchip!

A microchip is the best way to ensure that your puppy returns to you in case he ever gets lost. It's also used as proof of ownership if the need arises. The medical procedure is simple: A needle is used by a veterinarian to insert the microchip at the back of the dog's neck. This chip can then be scanned using a normal scanner which encodes the chip number. This number is linked to your contact details which are already in the maker's database.

If you adopted your puppy from a shelter or a reliable breeder, then most likely he has already been microchipped, and all you now need to do is to visit the company with the information and have your contact details updated.

STAGES OF PUPPY'S LIFE

A puppy goes through specific stages of growth just as a human baby. To ensure that you know how to take the very best care of your puppy as he passes through these developmental phases, you have to learn all about them. Let us go through these stages so we can help your puppy grow up healthy and strong.

Newborn to 2 weeks old - When puppies are born, they are unable to do anything for themselves. Their eyes are closed and they cannot hear. Mom needs to keep them warm as they cannot control how hot or cold they get. Mom even has to help them to pass waste. At this time you need to be very gentle with them so that they can begin to link humans with good experiences.

2 to 4 weeks - Puppies will start to stand on their own now. They are no longer crawling around and are noticeably stronger. They can already be seen interacting with the others in the litter and at about 3 weeks, they start wagging their tails. This is the stage where you can start allowing them a little freedom to explore in a safe way and a safe place as this will encourage confidence in them.

4 to 8 weeks - The weaning process begins and the puppy can now be introduced to solid food. You can now begin to see traits unique to her. Now she is beginning to be curious about everything around her as she now can use all her senses. This is the time you need to keep her safe as nothing is safe from her sharp little teeth and paws.

This is the best time to start routines such as regular grooming and cleaning as he is starting to develop a close bond with you, thus will also develop strong and positive connections to these processes.

This is the stage at which your puppy should also get started on the first set of vaccines and also get microchipped.

Puppies generally go to their adopted families from between 7 to 12 weeks old. If there is no record of him being vaccinated as yet at this point, create a vaccine schedule immediately with your veterinarian.

8 to 12 weeks old - Your puppy will come home to you at about this age. He will already be weaned and eating solid food. He will also be on a vaccination schedule. This stage is very important and sets the stage for what kind of puppy he will be for the rest of his life according to how well he is trained and loved.

12 to 16 weeks old - This is an active time for a puppy as he learns much of what he is going to know in life. He is introduced at this time, to both positive and negative experiences (consciously or accidentally) and thus if not handled properly, can be traumatized for life depending on the experience he was exposed to. He now gets used to veterinarian visits, training, and other places he is allowed to go to. As long as you ensure these are fun for him, he will grow up full of confidence and contentment.

3 to 6 months - Your puppy should now be finished with vaccinations and can now safely go around other people and other dogs. Training should now be continued so that you and your puppy will continue to understand each other more and thus continue to bond even closer.

Puppy is still in its developmental phase and so its activities should be closely controlled to keep him from injuring or straining growing muscles and joints. His vet will let you know the appropriate amount of exercise he should be getting at each stage.

He will be able to receive his rabies vaccine at about 12 to 18 weeks (depending on where you live)

Puppies can also attend their very first professional grooming. Be sure to keep the first visit short and not introduce her to too many things at once. He is now getting comfortable with scissors and blow dryers being used on him. He can get more thorough grooming at a later visit when she has gotten more used to the process and will keep still for longer periods.

6 to 12 months - Your puppy is now a teenager! Depending on your puppy's size, he may be fully grown at this point! (if he is a small dog breed, he will have reached full maturity, both physically and mentally by his first birthday) If he is from a large breed, he will still have more growing to do!

From 6 months old, puppies can be trained in competitive sports such as tricks and obedience rallies.

Most puppies also get to sexual maturity about this age (the largest breeds still have more to go) and you need to start discussing with your vet when to spay or neuter. This varies according to a dog's breed, age, health, and condition.

At about 6 to 14 months, your young doggie goes through another "anxious" stage. He is suddenly very hesitant around unfamiliar things and people. Even situations he has already been exposed to suddenly seem to be foreign and scary to him. He needs lots of reassurance and routine at this point and will soon be alright.

13 to 16 months - By this age, smaller breeds will have reached adulthood and larger breeds will be just approaching mental and physical maturity. Some puppies from really large breeds may not even get to this milestone until long past their second birthday! Your vet will let you know if your puppy has reached full maturity. If you are considering starting puppy on more active sports, his body has to be fully matured and his growth plates closed so that he will not be injured.

KEEPING DOGGIE SAFE

Puppy will depend on you to keep him safe from harm and danger. You must then learn how to make your home safe for him. You can start with one room and first check for any small items that he may chew on. Like electrical wiring, small toys, etc. These should be blocked off from your puppy. You can survey the area from the puppy's vantage point (down on the ground) so that you can be able to see any small item you may not have been able to see while standing.

REX! PUT KITTY DOWN! (TEACHING REX TO CARE)

Puppies should be trained to know that your small pets are also family members and so must be lived with gently and never teased. They should always be kept an eye on whenever they are around small family pets.

At first, the puppy should be kept on a leash when he is meeting that pet for the first time. They should be allowed to observe and sniff each other while you are praising the puppy at the same time. If your puppy starts barking and lunging, however, they must be separated as this can stress both animals.

Very importantly, you must keep in mind your dog's natural inclination according to his breed. For example, Some dogs are herders so should never be allowed to chase small pets.

Cats and dogs can live together very successfully and lovingly as long as these points are kept in mind.

SCHOOL TIME /TRAINING

According to Petra, puppies learn very quickly. The thing to remember though is that they also will learn everything! The good and the bad!

"I suggest starting training immediately," she says, "start by putting a collar on your puppy as soon as you bring him home. Then attach a leash and let him drag it around. Next, teach him to walk with you holding the leash. Housetraining should also begin right away, as well as crate training. Teach the puppy his name and any other thing you want to teach him."

Your puppy can also start attending puppy class as soon as at least two sets of vaccinations have already been administered. Here he will learn to socialize with other dogs and other people.

8

CRATE TRAINING

The use of crate training for dogs has become a common trend lately. It is done to help young puppies to learn to hold themselves for longer periods and also is a way of keeping them out of harm when there's no one to watch them. When it is used in the right way, crate training can be the perfect place for your dog and puppy to get some good rest. However, if crates are used for very long periods, many issues may arise. Little puppies may start using it as a toilet and big dogs will most likely become very agitated because of being confined for too long. If the crate is used in the right way, however, it becomes a most valuable way of training your dog and keeping him safe.

The First Time in a crate

All dogs will get used to the crate in their own way and in their own time. Your puppy or dog will need to see its crate as a safe place he wants to be. This is easily done if you make it into a comfortable and cozy space with soft bedclothes and his favorite toys. The first time your dog goes inside, the doors must be left open so that he will be able to exit and enter it when he wants to. He can be encouraged to enter the crate by placing a treat or toy he loves inside. If he stays inside and starts to play or eat, he should be allowed to do that with the door open so he can get out if he wants to.

The door can be closed for a few seconds at a time once he seems to be getting used to being inside. This can then be steadily increased to longer and longer times.

After your dog seems comfortable with the crate door closed, you may then increase the distance between you and the crate slowly. This must be done while your dog is relaxed. This process should never be hurried and can take as short as a couple of hours and as long as a couple of days. Whenever your dog enters the crate, you then say "bedtime" for example. This allows your dog to pair your word with the action of entering his crate. Your dog will soon be used to his crate and will be in a much safer space when traveling or any other likely longer visits at the vet or elsewhere.

CRATE HACKS

These are simple tips and tricks that will aid in making the crate a place not feared but loved.

- Make your doggie want to go into the crate by placing safe toys and bedding inside thus turning it into a nice, welcoming space.
- Before putting your dog inside, open the door for a few hours or days so that he can check inside if he wants to.
- By placing his most loved toy or treat inside, he will be persuaded to go in on his own.
- The door of the crate should never be shut until your doggie gets relaxed and calm inside.
- You may start shutting the door gently for a couple

of seconds at a time, while slowly increasing the time so long as he stays calm.

- Your dog may be offered a sturdy chew toy with food inside. This will ensure that he is not bored when inside the crate.
- Slowly make the distance between your dog and you longer.
- Your dog may have his meals in the crate so that he will see the space as a positive and enriching one and want to stay.
- Doggie should always have a way to get water while he is inside the crate.

WHAT NOT TO DO

- Your dog or puppy should never be forcibly placed inside a crate.
- The crate must never be used as a place to put your dog when he is "bad."
- The whole process of crate training should be slow and must be done at your dog's pace. If not, your dog will see it as a place to be hated and will refuse to go in or exhibit anxiety and aggression when placed inside.
- Never keep a puppy or a dog inside a crate longer than he needs to toilet. If this is done, he will be forced to use the crate to relieve himself and this will make the house-training go much harder.

- You should pay close attention to your dog's body language so you can keep track of his comfort level while inside the crate.
- A monitor can also be placed in a room so that you will be able to see how he behaves in the crate when you are not in the room.

9

DOGGY TREATS

You can find countless different kinds of dog treats all over the world. There are soft treats, chewy treats, harder treats, meaty treats and scrumptious cakes made just the way you ordered it for Rex. It can be quite a challenge to choose which treats to wow him with!

It is big business today and still trending upwards. It is estimated that Americans spent 38.4 billion dollars on pet food and treats in 2020, according to the American Pet Products Association. Dog lovers and owners today are increasingly concerned about the quality of the food and treats they are feeding their pets. They now want to know the ingredients, the origin, and the processing methods involved. In general, the same way people are trending toward healthier diets now, they also want to know that their doggies are getting the most beneficial and wholesome foods too and are also enjoying it at the same time.

We should not only be watchful of the quality foods and treats we give them, but we must also be very observant of the portions too. The fact that a doggie treat comes in a particular size doesn't mean he has to get it all in one go. It can be divided into halves, thirds, or quarters for him. Especially if you are using treats to train your dog, break them into bite-sized pieces.

COUNT DOGGIES CALORIES

Have you any idea how many calories your dog should eat daily? I bet you don't! You should talk to your veterinarian to find out how many calories he should consume daily. According to Dr. Ward, the treats you feed your dog "should not exceed 10% of your dog's daily calories."

Many dog-treat manufacturers do not include the calorie count on their packaging. However, the higher quality ones do. This should be taken into consideration when choosing treats too. We should also lean more toward single-ingredient treats as these tend to have fewer calories. Overall, keep in mind treats given throughout the day, whether at home or while traveling in order to keep a count on your dog's calorie intake.

It can be a bit harder to find the best treats if your dog is suffering from any health condition like diabetes or if he is just ageing. This can be fixed, however, by feeding your dog some vegetables. Most dogs absolutely love vegetables like baby carrots or celery and will be just as satisfied as store-bought ones. Plus, this is healthier. You should consider feeding your dog with food that will help their existing condition instead of those without any healthy addition.

WHY ARE TREATS IMPORTANT?

Any good trainer will tell you that you should have on hand lots of tasty treats for positive reinforcement when training your dog. Treats are powerful, handy and useful, and can be carried with us wherever we go with a doggie. We can find a treat that works with every dog. When we train with treats, the dog also associates what we are trying to teach with something positive and so will want to do it over and over again. We do not have to stop giving treats when the action is learned. Just as we love to receive payment for our jobs every payday, it is the same way dogs love to feel that they are a valuable member of our households, and treats do just that! It is a great reinforcer and it teaches your dog what works versus what doesn't.

CHANGE TREATS REGULARLY

There are so many different treats out there and this may be totally overpowering when it comes to choosing one. The main question to keep in mind is? 'Which treat/treats does Rex absolutely go crazy over? These are called your 'high value ' treats. These are the ones you need to use when you really need your dog to "get" something, or remember a specific command or stay somewhere he doesn't much care for. They do come in handy in times like these. One important thing to remember though is to always introduce something new to the doggie at home before feeding it when you go out. This will ensure that you catch any sensitivity issues which may make for a miserable trip out. In general, you will find the right treat for any dog! These are some of the various choices you can find out there.

- Dog biscuits: Old favorites for lots of dogs.
- Human food: Most of our food and vegetables are safe for dogs.
- Chews: A very good choice to keep your dog happy and calm, especially if you are going to be away for a few hours.
- Dehydrated: Mostly "one-ingredient" and meat-based.
- Cakes and cookies: Can be ordered from doggie bakeries or most local ones. Great treats for

birthdays or "just because you want to spoil your dog" days.

- Dental chews: Mostly just for helping to keep his teeth clean. Regular dentist's appointments are still necessary!
- Drive-throughs: Lots of these now offer items just for dogs. You may request them just as you request your meals. (You can order a Puppuccino at Starbucks and a Pup-Cup at Dairy Queen)
- Frozen: Most Supermarkets and Pet stores now offer doggie ice cream in different flavors.
- Lickables: Doggies lick these treats instead of eating them. This really helps with anxious dogs during an activity they do not like. For example while at the vet or while grooming.
- Grain-free: Your vet will tell you if this is necessary for your dog.
- Low-fat: Dogs are no different from humans when it comes to obesity issues. Always check calories when you are offering food to your dog, especially if the dog is not very active or if he struggles with weight.
- Oven-baked: Do it yourself or packaged, doggies love this.
- Soft and Chewy: Always a winner when it comes to older dogs with chewing issues. Most of the time they also have a high and very attractive smell which is also attractive to dogs.
- Refrigerated: Mostly single ingredients treats found

in the refrigerator sections of pet stores or supermarkets.

TREAT PORTIONS

Dog parents must be careful when it comes to treats. As usual, "moderation is key," Dr. Ernie Ward, author of *The Clean Pet Food revolution* cautions.

"The savvy health-conscious pet parent of today has to wade through a lot of marketing claims. If it looks good or if the dog just loves it, I'm going to give him more and more and more." He cautions that this is a common and understandable response from parents but this can be detrimental to your dog's health. Obesity is just one scourge that we can be encouraging on our dogs if we are not watchful and spoil them instead.

10

IS THIS FOOD GOOD FOR REX?

We love to pamper and feed our dogs with treats and food made just for them. The latest trend in doggie foods is made up of all-natural ingredients for the health of that beloved ball of hair. There is no shortage of variety. Some of these trending foods and treats we can feed our dogs are:

Peanut butter

Dogs just love peanut butter. It is also rich in antioxidants and Vitamins E and B. However, vets warn us to be careful and not to feed your dog with peanut butter which contains xylitol. This can be checked on the ingredients list.

We must remember that peanut butter is calorie-rich, so we must always ensure that doggie is not getting too much of this. It is also best to feed him with all-natural and salt less peanut butter.

Vegetables

Green beans and carrots are very good tidbits for dogs who are a bit on the obese side. As usual, though, moderation is key. You will need to check for how best he likes them served, the time he prefers to have them, and how they affect his stomach.

If very little time is available, the vegetables can be fed canned. Ensure that they are rinsed a few times, however, so that the sodium content will be reduced.

Sweet potatoes

Sweet potatoes are rich in fiber, Vitamins A, B6 and 3. It is also a good source of magnesium. White potatoes, on the other hand, are starchy and can cause inflammation in dogs. Sweet potatoes can be given to your dog raw. This will provide him with the most nutrients possible. It's best to serve it pureed or mashed as this will help in the assimilation of nutrients and also decreases the likelihood of a blockage of the intestines. It can also be boiled, baked, or roasted for a brief amount of time for nutrient retention.

Whole grains

Dogs really have no need for carbohydrates. However, if you want to feed it to him, complex grains like quinoa, brown rice, or wheat are best.

Bone broth (low or no sodium)

Broths are a great and tasty way to get sick dogs to eat while at the same time getting them hydrated. Bone broth is also rich in collagen, gelatin, magnesium, and glucosamine. Just ensure that when you feed him with this, the sodium is removed and that it does not contain onions. Bone broth can be given by itself, drizzled on top of other dog food, or frozen for a tasty treat.

Eggs

We know that eggs are a healthy source of vitamins A, D, and E, iron, and folate. The eggshell is super rich in calcium and the membrane is chock-full of glucosamine, collagen, chondroitin, and hyaluronic acid. It is good food for Rex too. He can have it raw or cooked and if the eggs are from a local organic farm, the shells can be eaten too. However, you must never allow him to eat the shells of eggs that are purchased at a store as it may have been cleaned with harsh chemicals that are not good for him.

Cooked Meat

Lean meat is good food for Rex. It does not contain as many fats and calories as meat that is not lean. We must still be careful of portion size, however. Meat must always be fully cooked to ensure that your dog does not get bacteria or any foodborne disease. Be careful when sharing deli meats with Rex, however, as nitrates sometimes lurk in them.

11

IS THAT MUD ON THE CARPET?

With all your well-laid plans, the inevitable is bound to happen sooner rather than later; mud has been tracked in and Rex is standing there wagging his tail all innocent! Just do this:

- For a small area on grout, you can use a simple pencil eraser. If this is hard to remove, special grout-cleaning products can be bought. You can also combine baking soda and water to a thick consistency and use a toothbrush or other small brush to rub it on the surface.
- Most prints tracked inside can be wiped away using a mop and warm water. If a cleaning product is used, the area should be cleaned again using plain water then dried.

- If the carpet is messed up, allowing it to dry first will make the cleaning much easier. This can be vacuumed first then blotted to dry.
- Simple fabric-softener/dryer sheets can be used to wipe off the scum and fur that always collects on baseboards. This can be done once every week.
- For a clean home, it is vital that you vacuum at least once every week. For best results, there are models that are made specifically for handling animal fur or hair. Get your puppy used to vacuums from an early age so that he will not see it as the enemy.

PEE AGAIN!

This is one thing you had better get used to when you get a puppy. There are various reasons why he will tinkle where he should not :

1. He has not been house-trained yet.
2. Puppy is having stress or nervousness issues.
3. He is just marking his territory! All sexes do this but males do it more than females. You can diaper his butt when he is at a new place and also get your spaying or neuter done as this will cut down on marking.
4. He may be peeing in the wrong places because he is ill. Get a vet to check this out if this is not the norm for him.

No matter how prepared you are though, you will have to deal with this eventually. You can do some things to help make the phase a little easier. Some of these are:

- Clean up pee before it has dried. This will greatly help with smells.
- Paper towels and old newspapers clean pee easily. Just keep blotting the area until all the liquid and dampness go away.
- Use clean water to blot the area lastly.
- If the pee has now dried, use a wet vacuum or a wet chamois to clean the area as above.
- A pet odor neutralizer can now be used on the area but be sure to wipe it clean with water and soap after.
- Call professional carpet cleaners.

OOPS! HE DID IT AGAIN!

Yea, the entire family just dotes on Rex because he is just so absolutely cute and lovable! However, all that cuteness has its trials too in the form of nasty messes called mud, pee and poop, so buckle up and get ready to clean! Don't worry anyway, we have got you covered with little tricks on how to best handle puppy's messes instead of seeing them as "stresses."

Being prepared is always the best way to keep messes from overwhelming you. Firstly, always have wipes on hand in your car. Anything that can be used to wash dirty and muddy feet can also be placed at the door. This can be just a container like a bucket or a basin. Towels should also be placed with them so your doggy's feet can be washed before he tracks all that mud and whatever else inside. More towels and /or another absorbent mat can also be strategically placed so that Rex has some extra surface with which to remove that dirt, and at the same time, dry those paws some more. A hairdryer can be placed in the same area too so he can be dried off when that dip is done.

In addition, you can also ensure that your puppy is wearing the correct kind of "shoes" according to the activity planned. Your dog should be trained before given shoes to wear and can be given high-reward treats to sweeten the deal.

Please ensure that stuff like sand or salt is washed off carefully as soon as the puppy gets in.

13

START A REGULAR CLEANING/GROOMING ROUTINE EARLY

Keeping all that fur or hair from your sofa, clothes and just everywhere is really dependent on bathing and brushing the puppy regularly. Trimming too is of utmost importance. His nails are not the only part that needs trimming. Any hair that sticks out from among the footpads must also be trimmed. This helps with the cleaning, thus decreasing the amount of dirt that is picked up. Use a soft soap and a gentle shampoo to wipe his little paws and wash him at least once daily. You may complete this with a paw moisturizer or a doggie conditioner.

14

HELP! MY PUPPY IS A MONSTER!

So you brought home the sweetest little ball of hair on four legs and now he is making you pull your hair out! You need to nip it in the bud as early as you can before it gets harder. Just as a child needs to be trained to exhibit acceptable behaviors, a puppy needs the same push. He needs to be taught actions and conducts that you want him to exhibit, while at the same time taught that some behaviors are not acceptable. This can be achieved easily with consistency and order. Keep in mind these important tips and Rex will be the perfect little puppy angel you want him to be.

Early training is key!

Your puppy starts learning very early. The day he comes home to you is the day he should start training. If your puppy was born at your home, then he can begin early training as soon as he is able to see and hear. When you begin to teach the puppy the behaviors that you need to see from this age, he will grasp them in no time. This is way easier than having to rectify incorrect ones later.

His environment is important

Puppies can smell up to 100,000 times better than humans and so, of course. They use their noses more to learn and understand the world around them. More often than not, whatever he smells will also be taken in his little mouth, This is the reason you have to make his surroundings safe for him when he comes home. Most behaviors we see puppy practices are rather typical puppy behaviors and puppies should never be punished for them. Instead, he should be refocused on more appropriate behaviors we would rather see him exhibit.

15

PUPPY PRACTICES YOU COULD DO WITHOUT!

PLAYFUL NIPPING

When the puppy was with his littermates, they would bite and playfully fight with each other. This behavior is important as it teaches them many essential skills. He still has this tendency when he is now living with you. Incidentally, when you roughhouse it with him and find it funny when he uses his sharp little teeth on your toes, you are encouraging this biting and will find it harder to stop this later on.

It is also important, however, to allow the puppy to spend time with other puppies so that he can indulge in these normal puppy actions. We can also refocus their energy on a tug-of-war game or frisbee which will keep us from being nipped for a while at least!

Chewing everything in sight

Just like human babies, puppies will pick up everything around him in his mouth. This is their way of learning about their world. This is the time you need to ensure that what he does pick up will not hurt him. It is at this stage that you need to offer the puppy suitable chews and toys so he will learn that these are what he should chew on, rather than the rug or your shoes. As long as this is consistently done, his chewing habits will be gone pretty soon.

Get down boy!

It is an instinctive and usual practice for puppies to jump all over each other when they are in a litter. To your puppy, this behavior is a normal part of his play. When puppy then runs on his short little legs and happily hurl himself into Mommy's lap, everyone laughs and clap their hand with glee at the sheer cuteness of it all, but what you are doing is telling puppy that it is ok for him to do this and he will certainly do it again and again until it has become a part of him.

Training goes a long way here. If we ignore him when he jumps on us and continually reward or praise him when his feet are all down, he will start keeping his feet all down in order to receive the treat again and again. Puppies are smart and will keep doing whatever he sees as rewarding, so do not look at him or talk to him at all whenever he jumps on you. Treat him as soon as he is down and in no time, his jumping will stop. However, this must be constantly reinforced until he learns it well.

CAN MY DOGGIE COME TOO?

I t is a common sight to see dogs accompanying families on vacations. These friendly adorable pets enjoy running on the beach, licking a cone in an ice-cream shop, sightseeing, or examining new scents and sights on the camping grounds or hiking trail. The fact though, is that many dogs become completely stressed while traveling. So before planning that vacation for you and Rex, you must think carefully about a number of things. Here are a few:

Does your dog enjoy new faces, new places, and new scents with no fuss? Is he anxious in new surroundings? What does he do when strangers greet him?

If your answers were mostly negative, then your dog may not do well on a trip to Jamaica with you. Don't cry! There are special, targeted activities and training that's made for dogs like yours. There are scent-work classes and trick-training exercises and many others to increase his belief in himself and make him into a doggie travel king.

TRAVEL DAY

Make sure your dog is calm and relaxed whenever he is in your car if a car is what you will travel in. Be certain also that he is safely fastened in a verified crash-tested carrier or harness because we all know that unfortunate events happen on the road sometimes.

Your dog can be helped to get used to traveling by taking him with you when you are going short distances to places that you know he will enjoy, like the park or a hiking trail. These distances can be increased over time.

Take your doggy with you when you are eating out at a restaurant or an outdoor cafe. This is great practice and will give you an idea as to how he will respond in new environments. On these practice runs, ensure you have his favorite blanket and a plastic, wooden, or rubber travel bowl. Let him practice settling down on his blanket in these places. This will allow him to feel a 'familiarity' everywhere he goes and thus keeps him relaxed and calm on the trip. Each time he stays calm in an unfamiliar space, make sure he is amply rewarded.

Always ensure that you find out the policy of a hotel before booking as each hotel varies. Some will allow unattended pets while some will not. This way, if you want to attend an event where he is not allowed, he can snuggle up and sleep on his own until you return to the room. Please remember to leave the "Do Not Disturb" sign hanging!

FINALLY

Do consider a weekend getaway as practice before the big trip. This will show you areas that your dog needs working on, or it may just show you that your dog is ready to hit the road!

Remember to pack additional food for him with the rest of his travel stuff. The brand of food he loves may not be available where you are going and this may cause him to get anxious and spoil your trip. Apart from that, the long travel may upset his stomach, and food that's new to him may just make that matter worse.

Make sure you have a copy of his vaccination records and your vet's contact information. Also, ensure that your dog's microchip and tags are current.

Most importantly, to the best of your ability, make sure that his trip will be a good one that he enjoys. If he really enjoyed that first trip, he will be waiting in the car each time you take up the keys.

17

WANT A CHEERFUL AND INTELLIGENT DOGGIE?

Who doesn't? Here are some ways you can make that pooch into a quality best friend:

- **_DON'T RUSH YOUR WALKS WITH YOUR DOG-_** Give him as much time as he needs to pause and check out scents galore. Remember, your dog learns about the world mostly with his mouth and nose. As a matter of fact, that area of a dog's brain that controls smells is 40% larger than ours. They also have over 300 million scent receptors while humans have just 6 million. This means that your dog uses these walks as an important learning class and will want to get as much out of it as he can. Let him! Also, take some small pieces of treats with you and place them in the grass all over so your doggie can forage with her nose.

- ***BOND WITH YOUR DOG*-** When taking your dog for a walk, leave your phone at home if you can. Help him to focus on the sights and sounds around him if he is being hyperactive. Allow him to be present and not just be barking and racing ahead.

- ***TRY DIFFERENT ROUTES*** - This doesn't have to be very far away. It can be just a street away that you do not normally use, or the meadow behind the old church you have never checked out. Just go in a new direction and captivate your pup's senses all over again.

- ***TRAINING TIMES MUST BE A HAPPY TIME FOR HIM*** - Research shows that an adult dog can hold his attention for up to 30 minutes. A puppy, however, will focus on something if it interests him, for just under a minute. He will return to it afterward but will again wander quickly. This means that if training times are too long, your puppy will just get bored and learn nothing.

- **LINK COMMANDS WITH INSTANT OUTCOMES** - Your dog learns the words "come," "walk'" or "treat" because they are always followed by an action he has come to know and love. You can gradually broaden your dog's list of words by constantly linking them together with more desirable outcomes that he knows and understands. You will be amazed at how fast he picks up.

- *YOUR DOG CAN BE TAUGHT NAMES FOR OBJECTS*- This is done through consistent repetition. You may teach him to retrieve 2 toys at a time. Ensure you are using treats to reward him when he retrieves toys. This will take a bit of practice but will eventually be done.

- *COOCHY-COOCHIE COO* ! - Just as baby talk is attractive to human babies, puppies also find it magical and reassuring. How we say things and the tone we use with them are of utmost importance. A study has shown that dogs react positively to cheerful higher-pitched voices like the ones we use when talking to babies.

- *HAND SIGNALS* - Your dog uses his eyes to learn as well. You can link specific signals to specific orders and your dog will soon be able to differentiate them. You must be very unvarying with your signals however, the same signal must always mean the same action.

- *TRAIN HIM* - Teaching your dog tricks is a great way to increase his confidence. You should begin with stuff you know your dog already loves doing with you. For example, If you have a doggie that likes using his paws a lot, then start by teaching waving tricks, shaking hands, and waving.

- *HE CAN PLAY BRAIN GAMES TOO* - There are mind/brain games out there for every dog. This can be paired with treats too for an awesome experience.

18

REX AND HIS NEW HUMAN BABY SIBLING!!

You have enjoyed all this time with your doggie and he has cemented himself into your heart and family forever. Now another bundle of joy is on the way, a baby! In all the excitement and preparation for Rex's new sister, you cannot afford to leave him out. A dog must be carefully prepared when a new baby is added to his home. This is a total stranger to him and he has to get used to someone else in his space. Let us talk about what you need to know and do for a smooth introduction of Rex to Anna.

1 to 3 months of pregnancy

There are many behaviors your dog needs to master when a new baby is coming to your home. It may be funny to you when he jumps all over you, but will he do that to a newborn baby? He is sometimes allowed to snatch his favorite treat from your hands or plate but won't he do the same to a toddler? Does he bite or growl when someone approaches him while eating? Does your dog "come", "sit", "stay," or "leave it" when told only once?

Rex may need to be taught or re-taught some basics before the baby comes. It is imperative that he knows the new rules and expectations in time so that by the time the baby arrives, he will have already been practicing them. It will stress both yourself and your dog if you wait until the baby comes and then expect him to understand why it is suddenly not ok for him to jump on the sofa. Train him for the entrance of this baby, and you will have a smooth introduction and bond.

4 to 6 months of pregnancy

Your dog should be training routinely now so that he will be dependably trained in time for the baby. You can start playing baby sounds for your dog. There are CDs available with these sounds and this should be played throughout the day while giving your dog treats. This will ensure that he will associate the baby with positive things.

If the baby's nursery area will be off-limits to Rex, you can start getting him used to staying away from that area from now. Install baby gates at this time also. The baby stuff should be set up at this stage so that your dog will get used to them being around. They should be turned on and used in the way they will be when the baby comes. If you are able to, let your dog become familiar with babies and small children and watch to see how he responds. He should seem relaxed and uninterested around them.

7 to 8 months of pregnancy

Tighten up on your dog's obedience commands. Ensure that he is now mastering them all and can hold a "stay" position for up to 30 minutes while you sit quietly. Make sure Rex is familiar with other persons who will help to take care of him while you are busy with the new baby.

If your dog is still showing signs that he will not be a good fit around a baby, you must make some very sad decisions as to who he will stay with until he is better fit to be around the baby.

9 months in your pregnancy

You must get Rex familiar with the smell of the baby while you are still at the hospital. A blanket should be sent home from the hospital with the smell of the baby on it. Let them wait until your dog is relaxed and allow him to smell the blanket.

When you are about to get to your home with the new baby, your dog can be taken for a good run so that he is exhausted and calm before the baby gets home. When he gets home, have his favorite treats ready so that he will link the new human with positive things.

Say hi in the same way you normally did as soon as your dog walks in.

Make time for your dog each day so that he will not feel left out and become anxious.

They are truly man's best friends! A boundless body of energy and pure, blind devotion. Your dog will indeed give you years of joy, companionship and love. Treat him kindly, love him well, and you will never regret taking Rex home with you.

So you have tons of valuable information at your fingertips to help you become the best doggie mama and papa in the world! If you enjoyed it all, why not tell me the parts that helped you best by leaving a review! Thank you!

CONCLUSION

Being a doggie parent is lots of work but as you saw, it can be a lot easier when you know what to do. Just as how you would prepare for a new baby, preparation is key for a new puppy too. When you are prepared and you have all the support needed, then your puppy journey will take you wonderful places. ! Have fun and enjoy the road ahead with your new little forever friend.

RESOURCES

https://smallbusiness.chron.com/start-tshirt-design-shop-11228.html

https://www.newfoundlandpuppy.org/cratetraining.html

https://www.petforums.co.uk/threads/not-sure-if-right-forum-but.532078

http://web.archive.org/web/20210307151628/https://www.pwrmeals.com/blogs/healthy-living/why-real-foods-are-more-than-a-trend

http://web.archive.org/web/20210118124650/https://pets.thenest.com/maltese-puppy-development-10674.html

HTTPS://WWW.EAGLEFERNVET.COM/NUTRITION-FOR-THE-GROWING-DOG.PML

https://labradoodlemix.com/how-to-https://labradoodlemix.com/how-to-train-a-labradoodle-training-guidetrain-a-labradoodle-training-guide

https://www.inquirer.com/philly-tips/best-pet-shops-philadelphia-20210514.html

https://www.medicalnewstoday.com/articles/https://www.reedanimalhospital.com/blog/creating-an-emergency-supply-kit-for-your-dog324453

https://www.reedanimalhospital.com/blog/creating-an-emergency-supply-kit-for-your-dog

https://wagwalking.com/training/train-a-pitbull-puppy-to-listen

https://www.news24.com/parent/Pregnant/Pregnancy_Journey/Getting_Ready/Babies-dont-bite-20081209

http://cover-mate.com.au/wyly/trained-german-shepherd-puppies.html